DISCOVERING MARS

The *Amazing* Story of the **Red Planet**

ISBN 978-0-545-83960-0

10 9 8 7 6 5   16 17 18 19 20/0

Printed in the U.S.A.   40

First printing, September 2015

Book design by Liz Herzog and David DeWitt
Photo research by Emily Teresa

DISCOVERING MARS

The *Amazing* Story of the *Red Planet*

By Melvin Berger

Revised and updated by Mary Kay Carson

SCHOLASTIC INC.

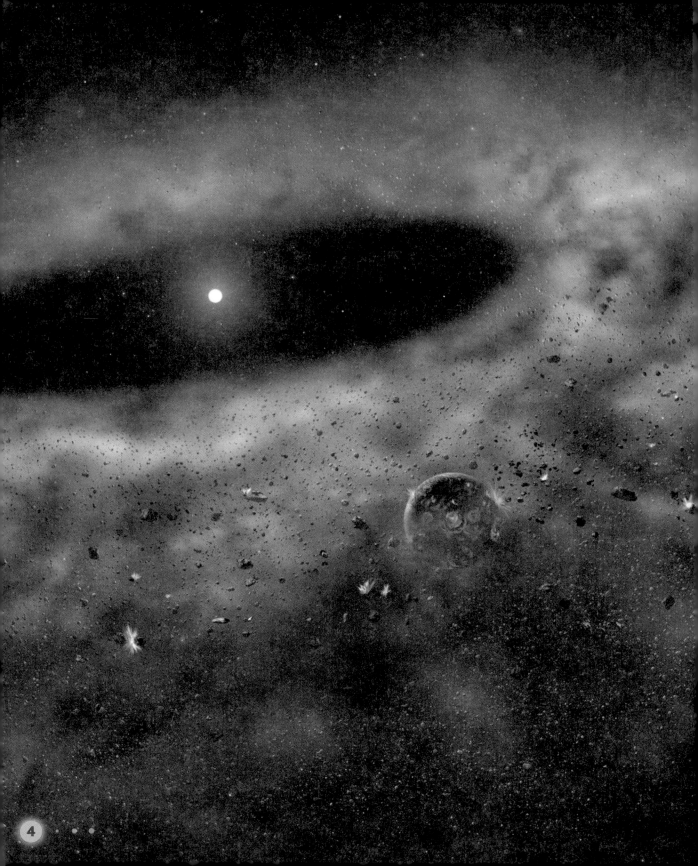

BIRTH OF MARS

Imagine going back in time about five billion years. Our galaxy, the Milky Way, is already very old. This spiral-shaped group of **stars** stretches across trillions of miles. On one of the Milky Way's spiral arms, a huge cloud made of gas and dust spins. The cloud gets bigger and turns faster, flattening out into a shape like a disk. Much of the dust and gas is pulled in toward the disk's center. The center grows larger, becomes heavier, spins faster, and heats up. Finally, it becomes a giant star, our sun.

Now imagine skipping ahead a few million years. Not all the **matter** in the spinning cloudy disk became part of the sun. Leftover bits of dust and gas still circle the young star. Those dust particles get larger as they bump into one another and stick together. Bits of dust come together to form larger clumps and then grow into rocky chunks as they keep knocking into one another. The biggest chunks form large balls, or spheres. These become **planets**. The planets continue circling around the sun. Each is tiny compared to the sun, the shining star in the center of the solar system.

There are eight main planets in our solar system: Mercury, Venus, Earth, Mars, Jupiter, Saturn, Uranus, and Neptune. Mars is the fourth planet from the sun. It is Earth's neighbor in space.

Not all the specks of light you can see in the night sky are stars. Some of the brightest lights are actually planets. Even before **telescopes** were invented, people could tell the difference between planets and stars in the sky. The steady points of light that change position from week to week are planets. Stars, however, stay in the same place and twinkle.

We can see five planets with the naked eye—Mercury, Venus, Mars, Jupiter, and Saturn. But Mars looks different from the other planets: It appears reddish!

You can see Mars without a telescope.
It looks like a pink or orange star that
remains bright and doesn't twinkle.

Mars

WHAT'S IN A NAME?

Long ago, the sight of a red-colored planet in the sky frightened some people. Red is the color of blood, so they feared it meant that war or death was coming.

The ancient Romans named the red planet after their god of war, Mars. The symbol for the planet Mars is a circle with an arrow coming out of it and pointing northeast: ♂ To earlier astronomers, this represented the shield and spear of the war god Mars.

Astronomers' view of the red planet changed once they began using telescopes in the 1600s. In 1719, an astronomer named Giancomo Minaldi first noticed large white spots around the north and south poles of Mars, but he could not determine what they were. Then, in 1784, three years after discovering the planet Uranus, Sir William Herschel, a German-born astronomer, turned his telescope toward Mars. With his improved telescope, Herschel was able to verify that the white spots were ice caps similar to Earth's.

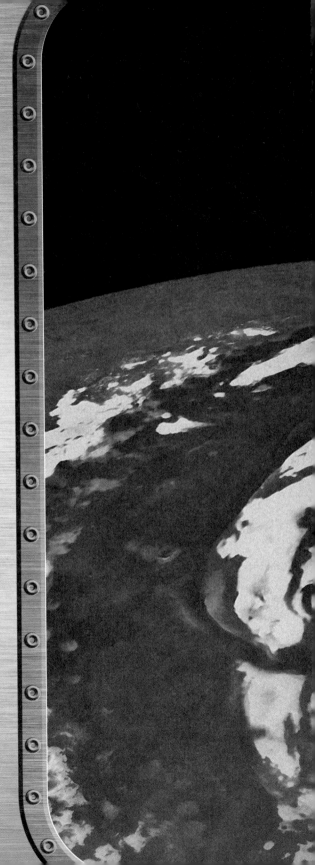

Herschel also noticed that the surface of Mars changed appearance at different times of the year. Some months, it was a darker red. Herschel wondered if the changes meant Mars had seasons or weather. The red planet seemed to have features in common with Earth. Could this mean there might be living beings on Mars, too?

The ice caps at the north and south poles of Mars shrink and grow with the changing seasons.

CANALI CONFUSION

Around one hundred years later, Giovanni Schiaparelli was looking through his own telescope at Mars. The Italian astronomer noticed about forty thin, dark lines on the planet. He called them *canali*. It's the Italian word for natural waterways, or channels, such as the English Channel.

Unfortunately, *canali* sounds like *canal*, the English word for man-made, artificial waterways. For example, it was humans and not nature that created the Panama Canal. The word mix-up gave some people the wrong idea. They thought that living beings had made the *canali* on Mars!

Pages from Schiaparelli's notebook show his drawings of the canali *he saw on Mars.*

PERCIVAL LOWELL

In the 1890s, the American astronomer Percival Lowell studied the ice caps, the changing surface, and the *canali* of Mars. Lowell convinced himself that smart beings on Mars built the canals to bring water from the melting ice caps to dry regions. He also believed that farming fields created the seasonal changes on the ground.

Lowell was a very well-known scientist, and many people believed what he said. They accepted the idea that humanlike Martians lived on the red planet, even though most scientists disagreed. It would take almost another century for Lowell's theory of intelligent life on Mars to finally be disproved.

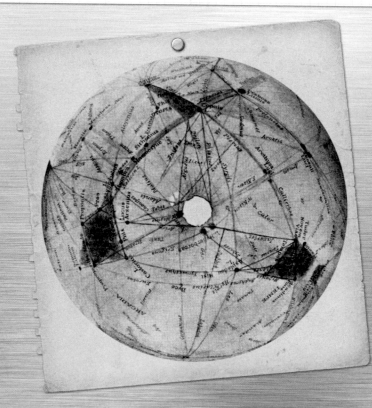

Lowell created this map of the canals that he believed were on Mars.

THE MARTIANS ARE COMING!

On Halloween Eve, October 30, 1938, many Americans were listening to a music program on the CBS Radio Network. Suddenly, the broadcast was interrupted.

The announcer read an urgent news bulletin. He reported that people had seen brilliant flashes of light coming from Mars.

After the news bulletin, the network went back to the music program. A few minutes later, the announcer cut in with a new development. In a concerned voice, he reported that a blazing meteor had just landed in New Jersey!

Soon, a reporter at the scene came on the radio. With great excitement, he described how Martians were pouring out of their spaceship. They were turning their deadly heat-ray guns on anyone within range!

All at once, the reporter's voice was cut off. Had the Martians killed him? Other announcers quickly picked up the story. They described the Martians invading New Jersey. And they warned that the Martians were advancing on New York City.

A HALLOWEEN PRANK

Some radio listeners panicked. A few grabbed their belongings, jumped into cars, and drove away. Others locked their doors and hid in basements and cellars. In New Jersey, a group of farmers thought they saw the Martian spaceship. They fired their rifles at a strange, dark shape in the sky.

By the end of the radio program, everyone realized it was all just a Halloween prank inspired by H. G. Wells's famous science fiction novel *The War of the Worlds*. But for a while, thousands of people had believed that Martians really were invading Earth!

The farmers who had fired on the "spaceship" were the most embarrassed. The morning following the broadcast, they found that they had shot several holes in the town's water tower!

The story made the front page of the Daily News *on October 31, 1938, the day after the radio broadcast.*

DAILY NEWS

FAKE RADIO 'WAR' STIRS TERROR THROUGH U.S.

"War" Victim

"I Didn't Know"

EXPLORING MARS FROM EARTH

Radio and television programs, books, and movies invent lots of stories about Mars. But astronomers have been making many exciting *true* discoveries about the red planet for centuries.

In 1877, the astronomer Asaph Hall made an astounding discovery. He found that Mars, like Earth, has a moon. In fact, he saw that Mars has two moons! He named them Phobos and Deimos, after the sons of the war god Ares in Greek mythology.

Deimos

Phobos

MARS'S MOONS

Phobos looks like a big, black potato in the sky. It tumbles about as it circles Mars. Phobos is the larger of the two small moons, but its widest diameter is only 17 miles. In comparison, Earth's moon is much bigger—more than 2,000 miles in diameter.

Phobos travels around Mars in a set path known as its **orbit**. The orbit of Phobos comes very close to Mars. It circles only about 3,750 miles above the surface of Mars, while Earth's moon orbits, on average, 240,000 miles away from our planet.

Mars's other moon, Deimos, has the same potato shape as Phobos. But it is even smaller: Its widest diameter is just over 9 miles! And Deimos's orbit is much farther away from Mars, on average, about 12,000 miles.

Phobos (below) and Deimos (right) are
probably **asteroids** that were caught
by Mars's **gravity** long ago.

TIME OUT FOR MARS

A year is the time it takes a planet to make one trip around the sun. The length of that year depends on two things: how far the planet must travel and how fast it's moving.

Planets farther away from the sun have longer orbits than closer planets do. Earth's orbit is 584 million miles around. But Mars, which is one planet farther from the sun than Earth, has an orbit of 888 million miles.

Also, Earth moves faster than Mars. Earth travels around the sun at a speed of 66,500 miles per hour, while Mars travels at a speed of 54,000 miles per hour.

The Sun

Mercury

Neptune

Uranus

Saturn

Jupiter

Mars

Earth

Venus

A YEAR AND A DAY

One year on Earth is just over 365 days. Because of Mars's longer journey and slower speed, it takes the planet much longer to complete a full loop around the sun. A year on Mars is 687 days.

This means that a year on Mars is nearly twice as long as a year on Earth. But a Martian day is only a little longer than an Earth day.

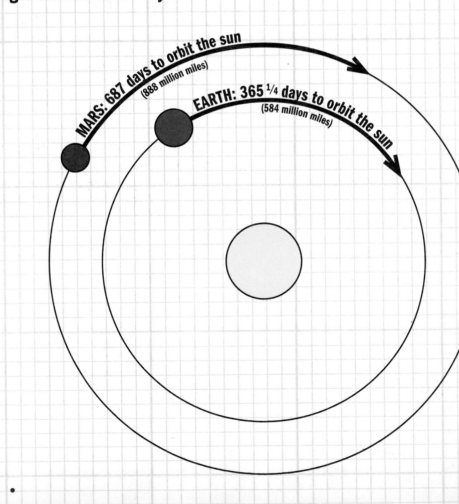

MARS: 687 days to orbit the sun
(888 million miles)

EARTH: 365 ¼ days to orbit the sun
(584 million miles)

How is that possible? Each planet in the solar system spins, or rotates, on its **axis** at the same time that it orbits the sun. A day is the time it takes a planet to turn all the way around on its axis just once. It takes Earth twenty-four hours to make one complete spin, so our days are twenty-four hours long.

Mars rotates on its axis more slowly than Earth does. Its somewhat slower spin makes a Mars day a bit longer than an Earth day, but not by much. It takes Mars twenty-four hours and thirty-seven minutes to completely turn around on its axis.

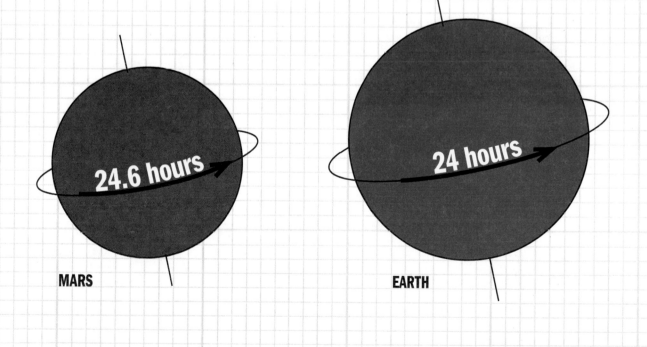

MARS

EARTH

A CLEARER VIEW

Modern astronomers have many new tools to help them explore Mars. With better telescopes and robotic spacecraft, they can see more details on the surface of Mars. Other advanced instruments can measure the temperature on Mars, identify what chemicals are on its surface, and pick out different gases in the planet's **atmosphere**. With this technology, scientists have been able to learn a lot more about the red planet.

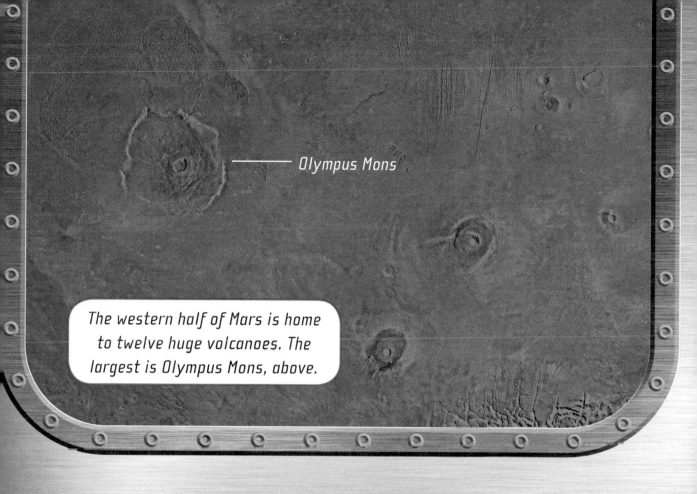

— Olympus Mons

The western half of Mars is home to twelve huge volcanoes. The largest is Olympus Mons, above.

We now know that Mars is cold, dry, and nearly airless. Scattered across its surface are many volcanoes. Some are giant, but none is erupting or still active. The hardened lava that covers the land is millions of years old.

In Mars's western half, or hemisphere, is a huge raised area. It is about 2,500 miles wide and rises 6 miles above the planet's surface. It's as big as the United States and Canada combined. Astronomers call this the Tharsis bulge.

VOLCANOES ON MARS

There are four giant volcanoes on the Tharsis bulge. The largest one is called Olympus Mons, or Mount Olympus. It is the biggest mountain on Mars and the largest known volcano in our solar system.

Hawaii's Mauna Kea is the tallest volcano on Earth. Compared to Olympus Mons, however, Mauna Kea looks like a little hill.

Each of the other three largest volcanoes in the Tharsis bulge (Arsia Mons, Pavonis Mons, and Ascraeus Mons) is over ten miles high.

At the peak of Olympus Mons is a 50-mile-wide basin.

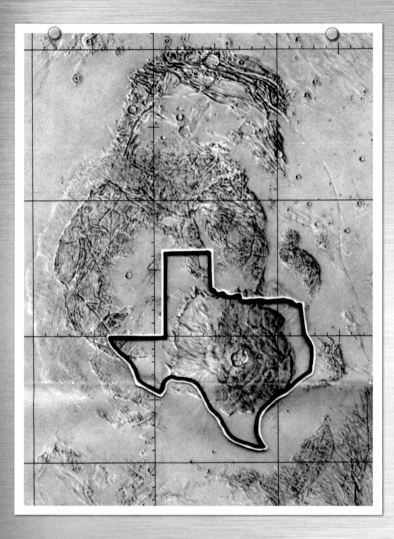

Olympus Mons is 15 miles high. Its
base is 375 miles across. That's nearly
as big as the state of Texas!

A view of the crater-covered Hellas Planitia area of Mars.

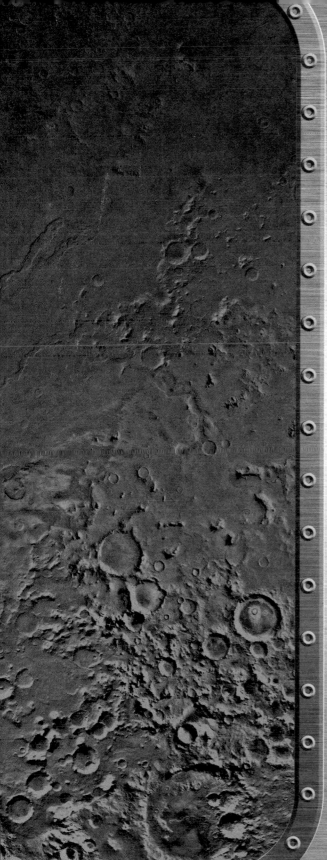

CRATERS AND METEORITES

The southern hemisphere of Mars has lots of giant holes in the ground, called **craters**. They were caused by falling **meteorites**, which are pieces of stone and metal that smash into a planet from outer space.

Some craters on Mars are enormous. The largest one is known as Hellas Planitia, which means "Greek Plain." It is one of the largest impact craters known in our solar system. It's about 1,400 miles wide, the same length as the distance between Chicago and New Orleans! And it is 2.5 miles deep, which is more than double the depth of the Grand Canyon.

THE MARINER VALLEY

The most fantastic sight in the southern hemisphere of Mars is Valles Marineris, or the Mariner Valley. The name comes from the *Mariner* spacecraft, which took the first photos of the canyon. Valles Marineris is a gigantic valley that cuts into the surface of the planet. From end to end, Valles Marineris is 2,500 miles long. On Earth, that would stretch across the entire United States, from New York to Los Angeles. From side to side, the valley is up to 125 miles wide. And in some places, it is almost 4 miles deep.

Experts think that Valles Marineris is a large crack in the surface of Mars. Since it is near the Tharsis bulge, the rising volcanoes may have caused the split. Landslides and flowing water might have helped dig out the steep walls, turning the crack into a giant canyon.

Valles Marineris is five times longer, thirteen times wider, and two and a half times deeper than Earth's Grand Canyon.

GETTING TO MARS

By the 1960s, scientists knew quite a bit about Mars. It was a cold desert world circled by small moons and covered in canyons, craters, and volcanoes. All this new knowledge made some people think about sending humans to explore the red planet.

But astronomers knew they still had a lot more to learn. They needed to get measuring instruments on or near the planet to gather more information. Just as they did on our moon, **space probes** (not humans) would be the first Earth visitors to Mars. A spacecraft going to Earth's moon is a baby step compared to the giant leap from Earth to Mars. Earth's moon is, on average, 240,000 miles away. But the average distance from Earth to Mars is 140,000,000 miles, almost 600 times farther.

Average distance from Earth to its moon: 240,000 miles

Average distance from Earth to Mars: 140,000,000 miles

THE FIRST "VISITORS" TO MARS

In 1962, **NASA**, the National Aeronautics and Space Administration in the United States, began a series of flights to Mars and other planets. It was called the Mariner program.

Mariner 4 made the first successful flight to Mars. NASA launched the space probe in November 1964. *Mariner 4* took nearly eight months to get near the planet. It came as close as 6,000 miles from the surface of Mars.

Onboard *Mariner 4*, a camera took pictures of the planet, and scientific instruments measured the temperature, gases, and **radiation**. All the pictures and measurements were sent back to Earth by radio signals.

MARINER MISSIONS

Early in 1969, scientists launched *Mariner 6* and *Mariner 7* toward Mars. Their missions were the same as that of *Mariner 4*. But *Mariners 6* and *7* were more advanced spacecraft. They came within 2,000 miles of Mars, and took much better pictures of the red planet.

Mariner 9, sent in 1971, was even more special. It didn't just fly by. It went into orbit around the red planet and circled it for nearly a year. *Mariner 9* sent back more than 7,000 excellent photos taken by its two cameras.

Mariner 4

MARINER DISCOVERIES

Experts carefully studied the photos taken by all the Mariner probes. They did not see any sign of growing plants or roaming animals. Mars looked lifeless on the surface and very dry. No liquid water, which is necessary for life, showed up in the pictures.

The Mariner probes also did not find any *canali*, or canals, of any kind. Then what had the early astronomers actually seen through their telescopes? Perhaps stretched-out shadows of long rows of big rocks and boulders. Or maybe chains of dark landforms on the surface blurred together to look like straight lines.

While there are definitely not any canals on Mars, there *are* some cracks in its surface. They look like Earth's dry riverbeds, which means that Mars may have once had lots of flowing water.

If that's true, the climate on Mars must have once been much warmer. But over thousands or millions of years, the climate changed. The temperature dropped and all the water froze. Today, scientists believe that any water left on Mars is ice, not liquid. The frozen ice caps that surround the planet's north and south poles are mostly made up of frozen carbon dioxide, not water.

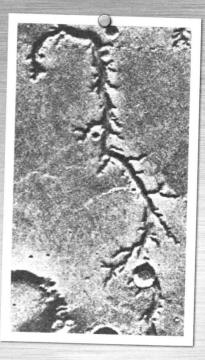

A photo taken by Mariner 9 shows a riverbed hundreds of miles long on Mars.

WHAT MAKES THE RED PLANET RED?

The surface of Mars is made up of dusty soil, much like the deserts on Earth. But Martian soil is red. It contains twice as much rusty-red iron as the soil on Earth. All that iron gives Martian dirt and rocks their reddish-brown color.

Scientists now know why Sir William Herschel saw the color of Mars change from dark to light. It's because of Mars's violent dust storms. The dust storms blow away the top layer of soil on the surface, which is light red, and expose the layer below. This lower layer is a darker color.

Raging dust storms are common on Mars. Powerful wind gusts send up huge towers of swirling dust. Sometimes, dust storms can cover the entire planet.

The rocky plains of Mars look like some desert landscapes on Earth.

COMPARING EARTH AND MARS

Mars is about half the size of Earth. A straight line through Earth from the North Pole to the South Pole measures nearly 8,000 miles. The same line on Mars is just over 4,000 miles long.

The pull of a planet's gravity depends on its **mass**. The more massive, or heavier, the planet, the greater its gravitational pull. Since Mars has less mass than Earth, its gravity is weaker than Earth's. The pull of gravity on Mars is a little more than one-third as strong as the pull on Earth.

Imagine a kid who weighs 75 pounds on Earth. With the weaker gravity, he or she would weigh less than 29 pounds on Mars. Walking around would feel light and bouncy. On Mars, you could jump higher, leap longer, throw farther, and lift heavier weights. You'd easily break Olympic records set on Earth!

On Earth, I weigh 75 pounds.

On Mars, I weigh less than 29 pounds!

There's also less air on Mars than on Earth. On Mars, the air pressure is a tiny fraction (11/100ths) of a pound per square inch. On Earth, the air pressure is nearly 15 pounds per square inch. The makeup of Martian air is also different. On Mars, 96 percent of air is carbon dioxide, with only a tiny bit of oxygen. On Earth, 21 percent is oxygen. This tiny amount of oxygen means that Martian air isn't breathable for humans.

Mars is also much colder than Earth. The average temperature on Mars is -81° Fahrenheit. On Earth, it's 57° Fahrenheit. The coldest spot on Mars is its south pole, where temperatures dip as low as -220° Fahrenheit.

EARTH VS. MARS	EARTH	MARS
Size (diameter)	7,926 miles	4,220 miles
Atmosphere (air composition)	78% nitrogen 21% oxygen	96% carbon dioxide
Number of moons	1	2
Average temperature	57°F	-81°F
Warmest spot	136°F (Azizia, Libya)	70°F (Equator)
Coldest spot	-136°F (Antarctica)	-220°F (the poles)

LANDING ON MARS

In July and September 1976, NASA blasted two new spacecraft toward Mars. *Viking 1* landed on Mars on July 20, 1976. *Viking 2* landed on September 3, 1976.

Scientists wanted to explore two different areas of Mars, so they set down the two Viking spacecraft about 1,800 miles apart.

Each Viking twin spacecraft had two parts. The main part, like *Mariner 9*, went into orbit around Mars. It circled the planet, taking photos and measurements.

The other part of each Viking was a small, crab-shaped lander. Each lander separated from the orbiter and parachuted down to the surface of Mars. Once there, both landers immediately started taking pictures. Radio signals flashed Martian landscape pictures back to Earth. The pictures showed a surface much like the deserts of the American Southwest. Most striking was the sandy, rusty-red soil and all the rocks everywhere.

Viking 1 *took this photo of the first ever panoramic view on the surface of Mars.*

Viking 1 Orbiter

A model of a Viking lander. Each lander, about the size of a small compact car, had instruments to measure and test the surface and atmosphere on Mars.

LIFE ON MARS?

The Mariner probes had ruled out the possibility of large living plants or animals on Mars. Scientists know that Mars is bombarded by deadly cosmic and ultraviolet rays, but they wanted to find out if there are any smaller forms of life on Mars. Could **microbes** like germs or bacteria survive near the surface?

The Viking landers were designed to search for tiny microbes, which on Earth exist everywhere—in soil, air, and water. Each lander had a robot arm with a small shovel at the end. Scientists back on Earth sent radio signals to the arm, which scooped up samples of Martian soil. Then it dumped the samples into tiny laboratories onboard the lander. Each lab tested the soil in a different way and radioed back the results. Experts went over the figures again and again. Finally, they reached a decision. The samples showed no sign of microbes or life of any kind. Mars looked to be a dead world.

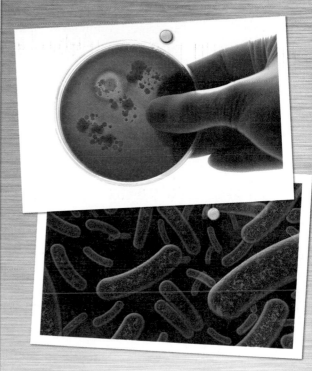

The Viking landers searched for signs of microbes in Mars's soil.

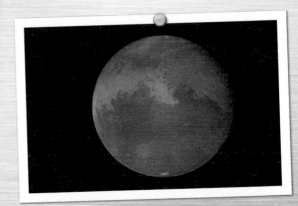

The samples showed no sign of microbes or life of any kind.

BOUNCING ONTO MARS

Two decades passed before another lander set down on the red planet. As *Mars Pathfinder* parachuted from space on July 4, 1997, giant airbags beneath the spacecraft inflated. The airbags looked like a huge tumbling cluster of beach balls! The *Mars Pathfinder* bounced before slamming safely onto the planet's surface at 30 miles per hour. After rolling to a stop, its airbags deflated. Then the spacecraft's three sides unfolded. Inside was the real star of the show, *Sojourner*.

This illustration shows how giant airbags helped protect the spacecraft as it bounced onto the rough surface of Mars.

A NEW ROVER

Sojourner was a rover with six wheels and topped with a flat solar panel. It was about the size of a microwave oven and weighed twenty-three pounds. *Sojourner* was the first mobile spacecraft ever on another planet! While *Pathfinder*'s camera took pictures and communicated with Earth, *Sojourner* rolled down a ramp and went exploring.

Mars Pathfinder's *camera takes a photo of Sojourner. The white fabric is the deflated airbags.*

SOJOURNER GOES EXPLORING

NASA scientists, using remote controls, steered *Sojourner* from Earth. Engineers carefully planned its path around boulders and over dust. Controllers sitting at computers (like the one pictured in the photo below) used joysticks and 3-D goggles to slowly maneuver the rover across the surface of Mars.

For twelve weeks, the little rover drove around, checking out nearby rocks. *Sojourner* analyzed their **minerals** and gases, and took close-up pictures. The rover discovered a rock that came from a volcano. Other rocks it studied were once underwater in a riverbed of some kind. Mars must have once been a wetter place, and likely warmer, too. It was clear that Mars still had mysteries that needed solving.

Sojourner checks out a big rock named Yogi, in July 1997.

WATCHING OVER MARS

Generations of spacecraft have orbited Mars—and still do. These circling robotic space probes aren't as famous as rovers. Most people don't know them by name. But much of what we know about Mars comes from the workhorse spacecraft that continually circle the red planet.

These orbiters have mapped Mars's surface. They've shown us canyons and craters, ice caps and volcanoes. Orbiters also make maps of what's not visible. They reveal the red planet's **magnetism**, gravity, mineral deposits, and elements. Mission planners choose landing sites for roving spacecraft based on the maps and discoveries of the orbiters.

Mars Reconnaissance Orbiter's *mission focuses on Mars's past water. It has taken amazing images of ancient gullies, dried lake beds, and washed-out canyons like this one in Newton Crater.*

COMMUNICATING WITH EARTH

Orbiting spacecraft serve as communication satellites during lander missions, too. A rover's small antenna can't send pictures and data all the way back to Earth. Mars orbiters gather the rover's information and relay it back to us.

Spacecraft high above Mars's surface also study the planet's atmosphere, clouds, dust storms, weather, and seasons. Their view from above shows Mars as a whole planet. The big picture helps explain Mars's surface better than the small, detailed snapshots from a few landing sites can.

Mars Global Surveyor created this color-coded map of Mars in 1999. The blue areas are lowlands and crater basins. The red areas are mountains and other highlands.

ROCK HUNTING ON MARS

Sojourner's success paved the way for a longer rover mission. The Mars Exploration Rover (MER) program planned to put two rovers on Mars for ninety days of exploration. The twin rovers named *Spirit* and *Opportunity* ended up roaming the red planet for more than a decade! Their discoveries over the years have changed how scientists think about Mars.

The MER rovers are golf-cart size—quite big compared to *Sojourner*. They have larger wheels and can travel farther and faster. MER rovers have better cameras and more instruments, too. Plus, each rover has a movable arm for analyzing rocks up close. A tool on the arm can drill into rocks or brush away dust while another tool detects minerals. There's also a microscope camera for taking close-up pictures of the minerals to study them in detail.

A model of the larger MER rovers, with bigger wheels and more scientific instruments for studying Mars.

SEARCHING FOR WATER

The MER rovers are made to hunt down specific types of rocks on Mars and study them. Engineers built the rovers to figure out the history of water on Mars. Was Mars once wet all over? Did it have only salty oceans or were there also freshwater rivers and lakes?

Water changes rock. Think of a round stone smoothed by a flowing stream, or canyons carved by rivers. Water changes the minerals and chemical structure of rocks, too. Oceans create different rocks from those made by mountain streams.

Since water shapes rocks and minerals, scientists can learn the history of water on Mars by studying its rocks. Once they analyze the rocks, scientists will more fully understand what happened on the planet in its past.

A view of some of the different kinds of rocks found on Mars.

OPPORTUNITY AND SPIRIT

The two MER rovers are identical, but they didn't go to Mars together. *Opportunity* bounced down on airbags on January 25, 2004. It rolled to a stop on a low, flat plain called Meridiani Planum. In 2000, the orbiting *Mars Global Surveyor* spotted **hematite** there. The dark mineral usually forms in watery places, so scientists wanted to get another look. It didn't take *Opportunity* long to spot the mineral. Little blueberry-shaped balls of hematite were nearby. *Opportunity* also photographed rock layers that had signs of flowing water. Scientists think the rover was seeing the long-ago shoreline of a salty sea.

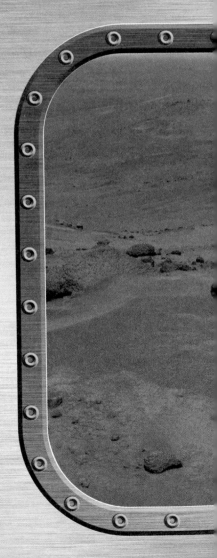

Opportunity *found these balls of the iron mineral hematite near the rover landing site. The balls formed when the soil around them was soaked in water millions of years ago.*

Spirit got to Mars three weeks before its twin, but landed in a less lucky place, Gusev Crater. After weeks of not finding any signs of past water there, scientists decided to move on. They sent *Spirit* off on a long-distance trip to climb a high hill. The view from the top was amazing. But even more exciting was the fact that the rover also found rocks that had once been under flowing water.

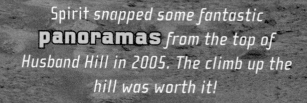

Spirit snapped some fantastic **panoramas** from the top of Husband Hill in 2005. The climb up the hill was worth it!

ARCTIC EXPLORER

From its orbit in 2002, the *Mars Odyssey* space probe discovered water ice near Mars's north pole. Scientists wanted a closer look, but a rover wouldn't do well in the dark arctic region of Mars. So they sent a lander named *Phoenix.*

Phoenix had two large solar panels for power, a digging robotic arm, and an onboard chemistry lab.

Phoenix set down in May 2008. Its cameras looked around at a familiar rusty-colored landscape of rock and dirt. But where was the ice? The cameras took a quick look under the spacecraft and discovered that the landing jets had blown away the thin layer of dirt covering the ice under *Phoenix*. Frozen water was everywhere below the thin soil!

Phoenix's robotic arm got to work scooping up soil and ice. Then it dumped the samples into the lander's instruments for analysis. The exciting results revealed that this was definitely water ice! *Phoenix* was the first spacecraft ever to touch water ice on another planet.

Measuring weather was another of *Phoenix*'s jobs. Its weather station recorded temperature, wind speeds, pressure, and humidity. The lander also observed frost, evaporating ice, and even snow falling from clouds.

Once the Martian summer ended, the amount of daily sunlight dwindled. *Phoenix*'s solar panels couldn't make enough power, so, as expected, the lander died. But not before it sent back the priceless pictures and data it had collected.

Phoenix captures a rare photo of a sunrise on Mars.

In the early morning, a thin layer of water frost is visible on the surface.

ROVING SCIENCE LAB

The Mars Science Laboratory (MSL) rover named *Curiosity* is the newest rover on Mars. It landed with high drama in 2012. A few minutes before the parachuting spacecraft reached the surface, it fired reverse engines to slow itself down. Then it hovered like a helicopter while lowering a dangling rover on a cable down to the planet's surface. Luckily, scientists were able to set the rover down exactly where they wanted.

Curiosity is a much bigger machine, twice as long and three times as heavy as the MER rovers *Spirit* and *Opportunity*. The MSL rover also carries its own power source. It doesn't depend on sunlight to charge its batteries, as the other Martian rovers did. It can work at night or inside shady craters.

The rover Curiosity used its arm camera to take this "selfie," or self-portrait, on Mars.

CURIOSITY'S MISSION ON MARS

Curiosity isn't just big and powerful. This rover is packed with new kinds of advanced scientific instruments. For example, it has a special **laser** that zaps rocks to identify their minerals.

Curiosity's mission is to find out if Mars was ever able to support life in any form. The rover is looking for the elements that life needs—nitrogen, phosphorus, sulfur, and oxygen. It is also searching for **organic compounds**. All living things on Earth are made up of organic compounds, which are the building blocks of life. In late 2014, *Curiosity* detected organic compounds for the first time ever on Mars! It's starting to seem like the red planet once had all the ingredients necessary for life.

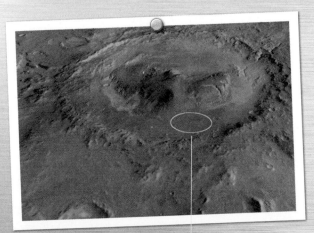

Curiosity's *landing site in Gale Crater.*

Curiosity *drilled into this mudstone rock and found Martian organic compounds for the first time.*

MARS SPACECRAFT EXPLORERS

(Years noted are time on Mars, not launch years.)

1965
Flyby probe *Mariner 4* sends back first close-up pictures of Mars.

1971–1972
Mariner 9 becomes Mars's first orbiter.

1976–1982
Space probes *Viking 1* and *Viking 2* each put a spacecraft in orbit and set landers on the surface.

1997
Mars Pathfinder and its rover, *Sojourner*, study rocks in the Ares Vallis region.

1997–2006
Mars Global Surveyor studies the planet from orbit.

2001
Orbiter *Mars Odyssey* begins mapping the surface.

2003
Mars Express begins orbiting.

2004
Twin Mars Exploration Rovers (MER) *Spirit* and *Opportunity* begin studying the rocks of Mars.

2006
Mars Reconnaissance Orbiter begins searching for water.

2008
Phoenix sets down on arctic ice.

2012
Mars Science Laboratory (MSL) rover *Curiosity* begins its search for life near Gale Crater.

2014
Orbiter *MAVEN* (Mars Atmospheric and Volatile EvolutioN) begins exploring the upper atmosphere and climate history.

Mars's robotic visitors landed on different parts of the red planet.

BIG MARTIAN QUESTIONS

Is Mars a **habitable** planet? Was it ever? Could it be made to support life now? This is what scientists want to know about our colder, drier, and smaller neighbor. NASA's Mars Exploration Program continues to investigate and is learning more every day. To understand the past, present, and future of life on Mars, we must try to answer these big questions:

- What is the history of Mars's rocks, landforms, and layers?

- What is the climate of Mars now and what did it used to be?

- Did anything ever live on Mars?

- Will it ever be possible to send astronauts to Mars?

The history of water on Mars is important for answering all of these big questions.

This model shows a version of what Mars could have looked like if it once had oceans.

NEXT STEPS

Dozens of spacecraft have been launched from Earth toward Mars. About half succeeded in their missions. After fifty years, the red planet has seen flyby probes, orbiters, landers, and rovers. So what's next for Mars?

More orbiter and rover missions are in the works. Scientists and engineers are also thinking about sending a drone airplane or balloons to explore Mars from the air. A probe or rover that could dig down or drill below the red planet's surface is also on the wish list. *Phoenix* proved that water ice is beneath Mars's soil in some places. Could fossils or other signs of past life lie buried, too?

An airplane or other flying mission on Mars would capture views lower than orbiters' but higher than rovers'.

MARS: DOWN TO EARTH

Scientists would like to study bits of Mars in laboratories on Earth. This would require a "sample return" mission, in which a robot collects some soil, rock, and air on Mars and then brings it back to Earth.

Sample return missions are tricky because there are so many steps to a successful mission. Each stage of the mission has to go perfectly, and there's a lot that can go wrong along the way. Samples have been successfully returned by robotic spacecraft to Earth from a space asteroid and from our moon. But Mars is a lot farther away. It takes an average of twelve minutes for a message from Earth to travel to Mars. That makes it even more difficult to solve any emergency problems that might arise.

A sample return mission would likely start with a spacecraft flying to Mars and going into orbit. Then it would release an attached lander that would set down on the surface of Mars.

Once on the ground, the lander (or its rover) would collect some air, rock, and soil samples. The samples would be sealed in a container and rocketed back up to the orbiting probe, which would fly it back to Earth.

The International
Space Station

THE FUTURE

What about sending people to Mars? Humans will probably travel to the red planet someday. But an astronaut mission to Mars will take a lot of work over many years—and billions of dollars. Many nations and perhaps private organizations will likely need to work together to send astronauts to Mars. The International Space Station (ISS), which began in 1998, is a cooperative effort among more than a dozen countries. The ISS provides a successful example of how nations can work together to further space exploration.

NEXT STOP: MARS!

First on the list for getting humans to Mars would be to build a spaceship large and powerful enough to transport people and at least three years of supplies to Mars and back. The trip to Mars would take over six months each way. The spacecraft would also need to keep the astronauts safe while on Mars, then launch off the red planet and bring them on the equally long journey back home. Finding ways to shield astronauts from dangerous levels of radiation is another challenge.

Meanwhile, the push to learn more about Mars continues. Every year, scientists discover new information about the red planet. The future is very exciting indeed!

GLOSSARY

asteroids–Large rocks that orbit the sun

atmosphere–The layer of gases around a planet or other space object

axis–An imaginary line through a space object's center about which the object rotates

craters–Bowl-shaped holes on the surface of a space object made by comet or meteorite crashes

gravity–The force of attraction between two or more bodies with mass

habitable–An environment with conditions that can support life

hematite–An iron-rich mineral that usually forms in water

lander–A space probe that sets down on the surface of a planet or other space object

laser–A device that makes a narrow, intense light beam

magnetism–The strength and properties of an object's magnetic field

mass–The amount of matter in something

matter–Anything that has mass and occupies space

meteorites–Rocks that fall from space

microbes–Microorganisms, or living things too small to be seen without a microscope, such as bacteria or viruses

minerals–Solid, natural, nonliving substances made up of chemical elements

NASA–The National Aeronautics and Space Administration, the space agency of the United States

orbit–The path followed by a planet or other space object around another object; to circle a space object

orbiter–A space probe that orbits a planet or other space object

organic compounds–Chemical compounds that contain carbon and are often found in living things

panorama–A wide and full view

planets–Large, sphere-shaped space objects that travel alone in orbits around a star

radiation–A powerful and sometimes dangerous form of energy that is transmitted in the form of rays, waves, or a stream of particles

space probes–Robotic spacecraft launched into space to collect information

stars–Large, ball-shaped space objects made of hot gases that give off light

telescopes–Instruments used to study distant objects by making them appear brighter, nearer, and larger

INDEX